CW01508354

"Flamur has compiled all of this schol
informed, and captivating story ... This is an endlessly engaging
book, an accessible read on a significant historical figure."

—**Burhan Al-Din Fili**, author of *The Spectacular Escape*

"Herewith I would like to congratulate Flamur for this essential
work. It is important to find out how the Mongols embraced Islam
and spread the faith into Asia; what the challenges were and who
was responsible for such an important event. A great book!"

—**Stef Keris**, author of *Europe's Forgotten Ottoman Heritage*,
founder of Al-Muqaddima

"*Berke Khan of the Golden Horde* is an easy-to-read, concise story of
Berke Khan, the first major Mongol Muslim leader, and the impact
he had on the Golden Horde and its successors in the region to this
day. A perfect companion to *Ertugrul Ghazi: A Very Short Biography*."

—**Brandon Mayfield**, author of *Grains of Destiny*

"This is an impressively researched and intelligently reasoned biography.
Well-written and full of surprises!"

—**Naser Bresa**, professor, author of *Alo, komiteti?*

"In *Berke Khan of the Golden Horde*, Flamur delivers a meticulously
detailed account of Berke Khan, a medieval Muslim leader whose
courage to embrace Islam led to profound historical shifts. Through
a well-crafted narrative, Flamur presents Berke Khan as not only a
strong leader but also a timeless role model for modern Muslims,
illustrating how faith can transform both individual lives and the
course of history."

—**Laureta Rexha**, author of *When My Absence Becomes a Moon*

**Also by Flamur Vehapi**
*The Book of Great Quotes*, 2025 (2nd ed.)
*The World According to Sami Frashëri*, 2024
*Kosovo: A Brief Chronology*, 2023
*Verses of the Heart: Poems*, 2021
*Ertugrul Ghazi: A Very Short Biography*, 2021
*The Book of Albanian Sayings: Cultural Proverbs*, 2017
*Peace and Conflict Resolution in Islam*, 2016
*A Cup with Rumi: Poems*, 2015
*The Alchemy of Mind: Poems*, 2008, 2016
*Sfidat Jetike: Poezi*, 2002

**Translations**
*The Expansion of Islam* by Sami Frashëri, 2025 (2nd ed.)
*The Album of Aphorisms* by Sami Frashëri, 2019

# BERKE KHAN
# OF THE GOLDEN HORDE

*The Mongol Leader*
*Who Forged a Muslim Khanate*

**Flamur Vehapi**

*with a Foreword by*
**Omar of the Orient**

*Impactful Lives*
Series

Crescent Books

Crescent Books

Prepared and Typeset by Erzen Pashaj.
Maps by Arbnor Rashiti.

Paperback:
ISBN: 978-1-954935-07-5

Subjects:
History | Islam | Mongols
Berke Khan | Golden Horde

Name of Series: *Impactful Lives*
First edition
Includes bibliographical references.
Text copy edited by Stella Williams
and Caitlin Dwyer.
Cover art by Lama Bayoun.
Cover design by Elipse Productions.
Decorative symbol used in this book is
from the flag of the Golden Horde.

Printed in the United States of America

# Contents

To my beloved parents,
as well as to Ryanne and Suhail,
the joy of my life.

❧

To the people of Palestine as well
who have been struggling to free themselves
from the shackles of occupation
for almost a century now.
*#FreePalestine*

# Note on Usage and Transliteration

Individuals experienced in translation and transliteration know the challenges of applying a uniform system to terms, names, and locations. Given the diverse origins of names in this work, similar Mongolian and Turkic names and words are transcribed as they appear in historical sources, particularly the *Secret History of the Mongols*, with occasional adjustments for clarity. But be aware that certain names might appear with slight variations due to their transcription from different scripts or dialects.

Most of the Mongol, Turkic or Arabic names, people and places mentioned in this book are often identified by Arabic or Turkish designations, which at times can be quite complex for the non-familiar reader to follow. Given that this book is written for readers without much background in the field, I have made efforts to simplify and regularize these names and terms wherever possible. For similar reasons, I have avoided the use of complex dots, dashes, and other scholarly conventions typically employed in academic writing to represent non-Latin alphabets like Arabic in the Latin alphabet (a name like *Dhia ʾul-Dīn ʿAbd al-Malik ibn Yūsuf al-Juwaynī al-Shafiʾī*, for instance, is presented as al-Juwayni).[1] There are exceptions here, of course, as is the case with symbols ' and ', which denote two Arabic letters ('ayn and hamza) clearly lacking close equivalents in English. Although I have limited the use of these symbols, they will be found in terms like the Ka'bah or 'Ain.[2] The name of the sacred book of Islam, the *Qur'an*, is also spelled with a diacritic, reflecting an attempt to more accurately represent the Arabic pronunciation of the word in the Latin alphabet.

On a similar note, when a widely recognized English version of a name or term is available, I have opted for that version. Therefore, I refer to Mecca, instead of the more scholarly 'Makka,' as a case in point.

Italics are utilized for non-English and specialized terms such as *quriltai* or *ulus* on their initial mention, with these terms also listed in the *Glossary* of terms at the book's conclusion.

Regarding chronological notations, CE is used for dates until the 800s, after which it is no longer applied. This book adheres to the Gregorian calendar for all date references only because the book is meant for a general Western audience.

ev

The Hijri (Islamic) calendar is lunar with 12 months, and its start marks the migration (Hijrah) of the Prophet ﷺ from Mecca to Medinah. This occurred in 622 CE, marking year 1 of the Islamic calendar.

To estimate the start of a particular Gregorian year (CE) in terms of the Hijrah year (AH), first deduct 622.5643 from the CE year and then multiply the result by 1.030684:

AH = 1.030684 (CE − 622.5643)

Similarly, to convert from a Hijrah year to a Gregorian year, multiply the AH year by 0.970229 and add 621.5643:

CE = 0.970229 x AH + 621.5643

For example, using the second equation for AH 1408: 1408 x 0.970229 + 621.5643 equals 1987.6467, with the decimal portion equating to seven months and twenty-four days, or 24 August. Indeed, the year AH 1408 started on 26 August 1987.[3] However, to simplify this process, there are many online converter engines available that can calculate the conversion between Gregorian and Hijrah years, and vice versa, as well as provide conversions for specific dates.

# Abbreviations

| | |
|---|---|
| **AD** | (*anno Domini*) Gregorian year |
| **AH** | (*anno Hegirai*) after Hijrah year |
| **Ar.** | Arabic |
| **c.** | century |
| **ca.** | (*circa*) about, approximately |
| **cf.** | (*confer*) compare |
| **d.** | died |
| **ch.** | chapter |
| **ed.** | edition, editor, edited by |
| **e.g.** | example |
| **Eng.** | English |
| **fl.** | flourished |
| **ibid.** | (*ibidem*) in the same place |
| **lit.** | literally |
| **MS.** | manuscript |
| **n.d.** | no date |
| **n.p.** | no place |
| **p./pp.** | page/s |
| **pl.** | plural |
| **qtd.** | quoted |
| **r.** | ruled |
| **sic** | (*sic erat scriptum*) thus was it written[4] |
| **Tr.** | Turkish |
| **vol/s.** | volume/s |

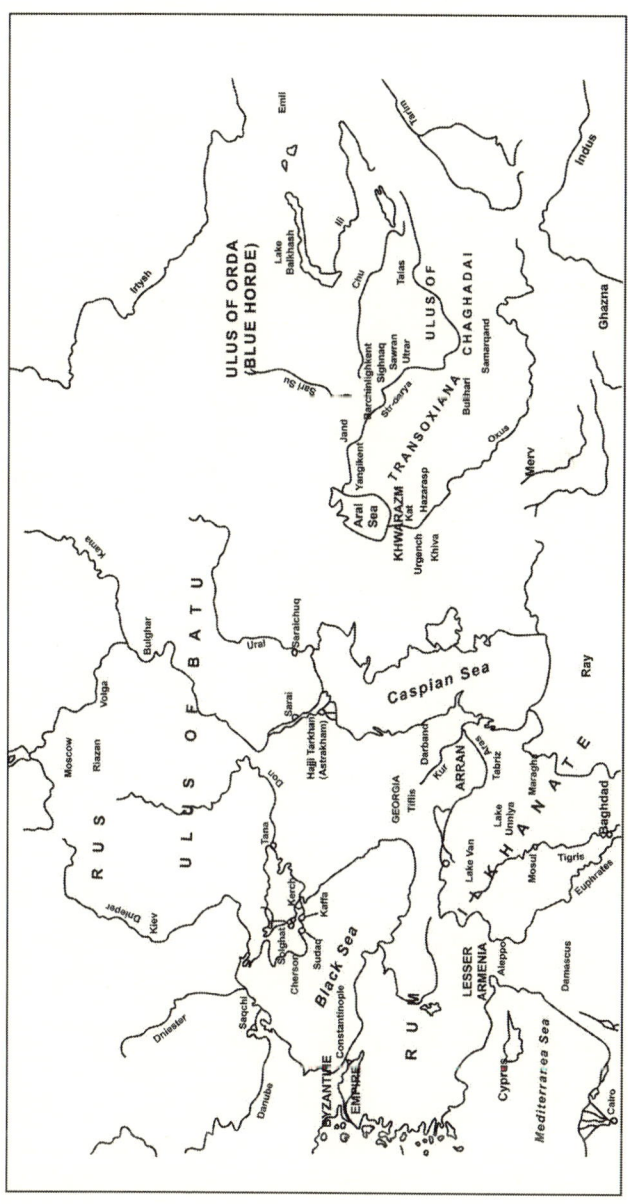

**Map 1.** The Jochid territories

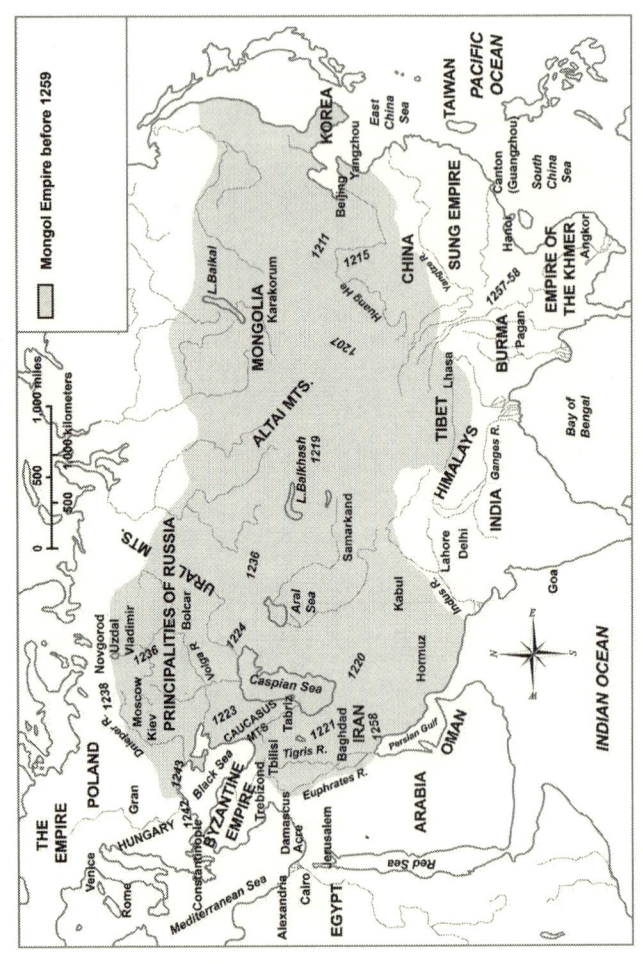

**Map 2.** The Mongol Empire before 1259

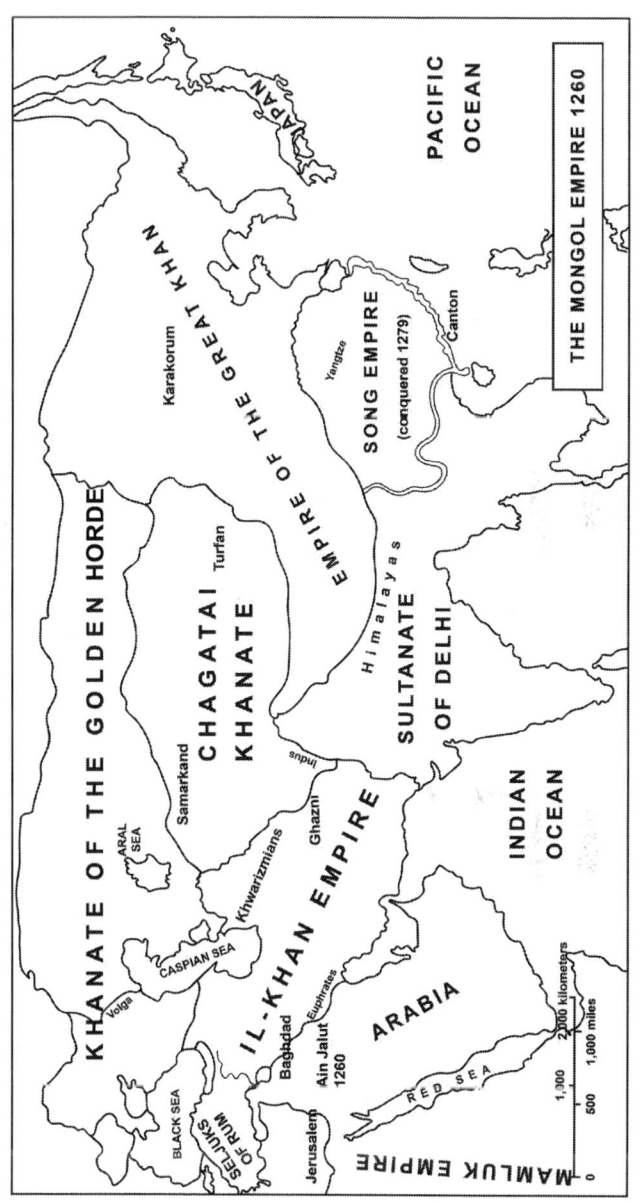

**Map 3.** The Mongol Empire in 1260

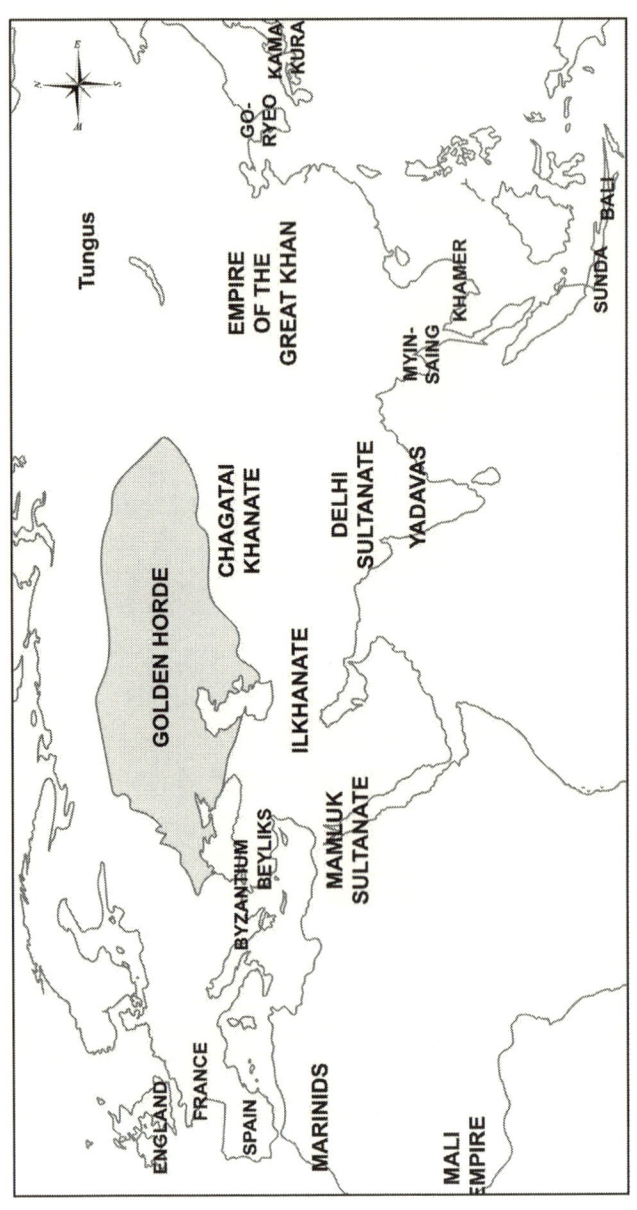

**Map 4.** The Golden Horde in 1300

# Foreword

Flamur Vehapi's biography of Berke Khan brings to light one of the greatest figures in Muslim history, yet often forgotten or unknown to many.

The grandson of Genghis Khan, Berke, holds a unique place in Muslim history. He was the first Mongol leader to embrace Islam, playing a crucial role in the spread of the faith across his empire. His conversion and subsequent policies not only influenced the Mongol Empire's stance towards Muslims but also established a significant Muslim presence in regions under his control, completely reshaping the Muslim world.

This book is more than just a history lesson; it's a personal mission for Flamur. As an educator with a deep love for Islamic history, he aims to educate both Muslims and non-Muslims about the rich heritage of Islam. And with his passion for teaching and his gift for turning meticulous research into captivating stories, Flamur makes the life of Berke Khan accessible and interesting to all readers.

**Omar of the Orient,**
Muslim Content Creator
www.youtube.com/@OmaroftheOrient

# Introduction

*"My Lord! Increase me in knowledge ..."*[5] – Qur'an 20:114

As is the case with many "eastern" heroes of the past, Berke Khan is not commonly known to many of us in the Western hemisphere.[a] If mentioned at all, at times his name is brought up in passing in relation to his family, and other times he is only referred to as 'the Mongol leader who converted to Islam.'

As for my own knowledge of this great leader, admittedly I was first introduced to the name of Berke Khan through *Resurrection: Ertugrul,* the widely known historical fiction drama based on the story of Ertugrul Ghazi, the father of Osman I (who founded the Ottoman Empire). Although the famous Turkish drama series does not strictly observe historical accuracy, in a few of the scenes Berke Khan appears

---

[a] The word 'khan' has often varied in meaning based on its context, serving as a title, office, form of address, attribute of rulership post-Genghis Khan's Mongol unification, or part of a place name. It is commonly used in Central Asia, North India, Pakistan, Iran, and Turkey. Its origins are likely Turkic, as it was a historic Turko-Mongol title from the nomadic tribes in the Central and Eastern Eurasian Steppe. For more on the peoples of the Steppes, see Taşağıl, *Bozkırın Kağanlıkları,* 2018; Harl, *Empires of the Steppes,* 2023.

as a powerful opponent, and later as an ally of the Seljuks and friend of Ertugrul Gazi, the protagonist of the show. The plot involving Berke Khan revolves around the geopolitical conflicts between the Mongols themselves as well as the Seljuk State and the emerging Ottoman state that Ertugrul and his allies struggled to establish. Berke Khan's character, however, is portrayed as a thoughtful, strategic and dynamic leader, reflecting his conversion to Islam and his conflicts with other Mongol leaders who often clashed with many of the weakened Muslim and Byzantine states in the region.

Setting aside the elements of historical fiction from *Resurrection: Ertugrul*, the portrayal of Berke Khan's persona, character, and the historical context depicted in the show is not very far from the truth, and these claims are supported by existing albeit scarce sources I have been able to access and present in this concise biography. I am well aware that what I have presented here is an incomplete picture of this great leader, people and domain, due to the scarcity of information available, but I am hopeful that more of this research will come to light in the future for those of us craving to know more. I hope you enjoy this brief read just as much as I enjoyed putting it together.

# Berke Khan and the Mongol Empire

*"God does not forbid you from dealing kindly and fairly with those who have neither fought nor driven you out of your homes. Surely God loves those who are fair."* – Qur'an 60:8

Berke Khan, originally a military commander and later ruler of the Golden Horde (a division of the Mongol Empire),[6] played a pivotal role in consolidating the power of both the Blue Horde and White Horde from 1257 to 1266.[7] As the grandson of Genghis Khan, he succeeded his brother Batu Khan of the Blue Horde in the west.[a] As we will later note, Berke Khan was instrumental in officially establishing Islam in a *khanate* of the Mongol Empire, which at the time was heavily invested in shamanism and other native belief systems.[8]

---

[a] The White Horde and the Blue Horde were two parts of the Golden Horde. The Blue Horde, also known as the Western Horde, was led by Batu Khan, and controlled the western regions, including parts of modern-day Russia and Eastern Europe. The White Horde, or Eastern Horde, was governed by Batu's brother Orda and ruled over the eastern territories, including parts of Central Asia. Over time, the two hordes merged, making up the Golden Horde. See Wolfe, *Batu, Khan of the Golden Horde*, 2020. Cf. Jackson, *The Mongols and the Islamic World*, 182, 2017.

As leader of the Golden Horde, Berke's military campaigns involved not only quashing external rebellions, but also consolidating power away from his cousin Hülegü Khan (Genghis Khan's grandson and son of Tolui), who headed the Mongol *Ilkhanate* in the territories of Iran. To this end, during the aftermath of the Sack of Baghdad by Hülegü, Berke formed an alliance with the Egyptian Mamluks[a] to oppose Hülegü's territorial and political advances (especially in the territories of present-day Azerbaijan).[9] In addition to his regional engagements, Berke supported his relative Ariq Böke against Kublai in the Toluid Civil War.[10] Despite his backing of Ariq Böke, however, Berke refrained from direct military intervention in the conflict, as he was preoccupied with his own war against Hülegü and the Ilkhanate.[11]

This period marked Berke's strategic maneuvering in the complex political landscape of the Mongol Empire, an empire that was mostly hostile to Islam and Muslims. That was soon about to change, however, with Berke's newly discovered faith, an event that slowly but surely drew a major portion of the Mongol Empire into the fold of Islam.[12]

Berke is also known as one of the few Mongol leaders who did not acknowledge Kublai (brother of Hülegü) as the Great Khan of the empire, which was not only due to the political and

---

[a] The Mamluks of Egypt were a military caste that rose to power by overthrowing the Ayyubid dynasty and establishing their own sultanate in Egypt in 1250. They were formidable warriors, originally slaves of Turkic, Caucasian, and other origins, who became the ruling elite. Before and during the time of Berke Khan, the Mamluks played a crucial role in resisting Mongol expansion into the Middle East. For details, see Amitai-Preiss, *Mongols and Mamluks*, 2005.

religious differences between the two leaders.[13] It was also about a long history of rivalry between the two princes, as well as their personal ambitions to consolidate power and expand their influence in the region, which eventually led to open conflict between their powerful households (the Jochids, led by Berke, and the Toluids, led by Hülegü).[14] Ultimately, this refusal to acknowledge Kublai as the Great Khan reflected deeper schisms within the Mongol Empire during Berke's time, highlighting how the once-unified empire had evolved into a collection of increasingly independent and ideologically diverse states.[15]

# His Family

*"Whoever is pleased to have his provision expanded and his life span extended, let him keep good relations with his family."*[16]
– Prophet Muhammad ﷺ

Berke Khan was a member of the Borjigin family, the ruling clan of the Mongol Empire founded by his grandfather, Genghis Khan (1162–1227). He was the son of Jochi Khan (1181–1227)—the eldest son of Genghis Khan—and the leader of the Golden Horde (the western part of the empire) which stretched all the way to present-day Europe.[17] As for the Jochid *ulus* (a gift of land provided to princes), where Berke was born and lived, Genghis Khan had established it in 1224/5 as a reward for his eldest son, Jochi, following a successful campaign against the eastern Kipchaks and the Qangli, and the conquest of Urgench. Jochi was granted an ulus consisting of territories west of the Irtysh River, which had been previously subjugated by Mongol forces led by Jebe and Sübedei[a]

---

[a] Jebe and Sübedei were two of the most renowned generals in the Mongol Empire under Genghis Khan. Jebe, originally an enemy warrior who defected to Genghis Khan, and Sübedei, a close and loyal strategist, were instrumental in the Mongol conquests across Asia and into Europe. Together, they led several key campaigns,

between 1220 and 1224.[18]

There is uncertainty as to who Berke's mother was since his father married at least four other women. Some have claimed that she was Khan Sultan (Sultan Khatun),[19] the captured daughter of a Khwarezmian *shah*.[a] Many historians have doubted such claims, however.

Although the information is scarce, it is said that Jochi had two daughters and 14 sons, with Batu, Berkejar, Bora, Orda, Shiban, and Tuqa-Timur being of his most commonly known sons; the last three are said to have been Berke's full-blood brothers.[20] Contemporary Persian historian Rashid al-Din, however, noted that Jochi fathered close to forty sons and had countless grandsons, leading to a rapid expansion of the Jochid lineage. Within just two generations, their family expanded to encompass several hundred members.[21]

As is the case with many figures of this time, Berke's exact date of birth is not well-documented, however, most sources point to sometime between 1207 and 1209. Others have indicated that Berke might have been born at least a decade after that, most likely during the Mongol conquest of Khwarezm which took place between 1219 and 1221. Although in the minority, the latter group of sources includes Minhaj al-Siraj

---

including the famous invasion of the Khwarezmian Empire and the unprecedented raid into Eastern Europe, where they defeated the combined forces of Hungary and Poland at the Battles of Mohi and Legnica in 1241. Their military genius and innovative tactics significantly expanded the Mongol Empire, making them legendary figures in the history of warfare. For details, see May and Hope, eds., *The Mongol World*, 2022.

[a] Khwarezm was a Persianate Muslim empire in Central Asia and Iran.

Juzjani, another 13th-century Persian historian of this period.[22]

Moreover, there is also very little information about Berke's early years and his youth. Some sources claim that Berke was nursed by a Muslim midwife, but the details are ambiguous on this matter.[23] We do know for certain that young Berke participated in the *quriltai* (council) for the succession to the throne of two of his uncle's sons, Güyük (son of Ögedei) and Möngke (son of Tolui) in 1246 and 1251 respectively, and that Berke's peacekeeping efforts prevented some internal conflicts during this crucial moment in Mongol history.[24]

As for his name, 'Berke' (also found as Bereke, Burge, or Birkai) is a common name among both Turkic peoples and Mongols. In Mongolian, 'berke' translates to 'challenging,' 'difficult' or 'tough.' Because of the name's historical and cultural significance, reflecting the long-standing tradition of naming children after distinguished figures of historical importance, the name Berke is still used in Mongolia and other Turkic lands to this day.[25]

## Youth and Positions
## Before Enthronement

*"Each of you is a shepherd and each of you is responsible for his flock. The Amir (ruler) who is over the people is a shepherd and is responsible for his flock."*[26] – Prophet Muhammad ﷺ

As already noted, we have very little information about the period before Berke became the ruler of the Golden Horde. However, like many princes of the Mongol imperial family, it is likely that Berke held various military and administrative positions under the leadership of his predecessors, including his brother Batu Khan, who led the Mongol invasions into Europe and established the Golden Horde's dominance in that region.[27]

During his campaigns against the Cumans in south Russia, for instance, Batu Khan assigned Berke as the commander in charge of the operations (Berke swiftly defeated and brought the Cumans under Mongol control in 1238).[28] Additionally, Möngke Khan is said to have assigned the lands of present-day Georgia to the care of Berke, clearly demonstrating that Berke was well trusted and very involved in the affairs of the empire before his khanship.[29] Moreover, after the fall of the Khwarezmian Empire to the Mongols, Berke served as a military general there.[30]

As for his preparation and development, Berke's upbringing in the Mongol nobility would have included extensive training in martial, strategic, and leadership skills, preparing him for eventual leadership roles (even though Berke was not in the line of succession for the Golden Horde).[31] His exact positions or titles before becoming khan, however, are not well-documented in historical sources, which instead emphasize his contributions and leadership after he ascended to power.[32]

## Conversion to Islam

*"Let there be no compulsion in religion, for the truth stands out clearly from falsehood."* – Qur'an 2:256

Although Islam was present in the vast Mongol Empire and its controlled territories prior to Berke Khan's conversion, the empire was predominantly shamanistic at this point, marked with a significant degree of tolerance for the various belief systems in the region, at least in its earliest stages.[33] By Berke's lifetime, the empire covered numerous Muslim-majority regions, particularly in Central Asia and the Middle East, where Islam had been well-established for centuries.[34] Naturally, the Mongols interacted with their Muslim subjects and allies, and undoubtedly many of them adopted Islam as their way of life.[35]

As for Berke, he most likely accepted Islam before becoming a khan, during his time as a general in Khwarezm, and he is often credited as the first member of the Mongol elite, and later ruler, to officially convert to Islam.[36] His conversion to Islam is validated in a number of accounts.[37] Marie Favereau, for instance, in *The Horde* describes an interaction between Berke and the Mamluk emissaries of the sultan of Egypt who visited Berke in his royal throne, apparently to verify the rumors of this conversion.

After some Mamluk emissaries on the orders of their sultan arrived at the banks of the Volga and settled their tents there, notes Favereau, the emissaries were taken by Jochid officials to their khan's tent. Upon meeting the khan (i.e. Berke), the emissaries handed him a letter from the Sultan, which the khan asked to be translated immediately, and the khan asked the emissaries a series of questions about their lands and leadership. The khan's guests were also offered gifts, and only after 26 days of their stay in the company of the khan and his court did the emissaries leave the Golden Horde following a reply they were given by the khan. Berke Khan had confirmed to them his conversion to Islam and agreed to an alliance with the Mamluks.[38] This was not the first or the last time the Mamluks and the Jochids interacted with each other; these exchanges were pivotal in transforming both the Horde and the Mamluk dominion in the region.[39]

Even though this account, and a few others, substantiate the genuine nature of Berke's conversion to Islam, what they don't tell us is how, where, and when the khan had accepted Islam.[40] Some have noted that Berke had converted to Islam in his early youth,[41] and others, as stated earlier, assert that he converted during his time as a Mongol general in Khwarezm as he interacted with the Muslim populations there, particularly the religious communities.[42] A widely known story, seemingly connected to the last theory, describes how Berke encountered a caravan of Muslim traders passing through Bukhara. After questioning them about their faith, he was impressed by their beliefs and ultimately embraced Islam.[43] Although it is very likely that Berke showed interest in Islam at an early age considering the Mongol involvement with Muslim communities in the region, the latter accounts seem more in line with the context of Berke's life, and most historians of this period agree with that opinion.[44]

Others more specifically indicate that Shaykh Najm al-Din Kubra's disciple, Seyfeddin Bakharzi (d. 1261), played a significant role in Berke's conversion.[45] Bakharzi, who taught in Bukhara (then part of the Muslim Khwarezmian Empire), is said to have earned the respect of many viziers, statesmen, and rulers in the region. During one of Berke Khan's visits to Bukhara, Berke met the shaykh himself and under his influence converted to Islam soon after.[46] If this were truly the case, the shaykh's significant influence on Berke and the role he played in Berke's conversion and ascent to the throne appears undeniable.[47] No date of this event has been recorded, but years 1252 and 1253 are often cited for this occurrence.[48]

As for the site of Berke's conversion, most say that it was Bukhara, but Saray-Jük (Sarayçıq), located in modern western Kazakhstan, has also been noted by the likes of Abu al-Ghazi Bahadur (r. 1643–1663), a descendant of Genghis Khan.[49] Although we may never know the exact year and precise location of Berke's conversion, both Ibn Khaldun and Badr al-Din al-Ayni affirm that Berke's conversion was directly related to the teachings and influence of Bakharzi, and the location of Bukhara had an exceptional role in the process.[50]

Be that as it may, soon after Berke proclaimed his Islam openly, most of Berke's tribesmen as well as his troops and *amir*s became Muslim;[51] so did two of his brothers, Berkejar and Bora/Muḥammad.[52] After the events, his family displayed Islam with pride, and it is said that Berke's wife, Jijak Khatun, had a tent-mosque that accompanied her every time she traveled.[53] A Hanafi jurist even dedicated a treatise to Berke.[54] Moreover, Berke's open embrace of Islam played a crucial role in aligning the Mamluks with the Jochid domain (as will be discussed later), simultaneously establishing the Horde's autonomy from the central Mongol authority.[55]

His conversion marked a significant turning point of the Golden Horde, as well as leading to Islam becoming more influential within various parts of the Mongol Empire.[56] However, this does not mean Islam was introduced to the Mongols for the first time at this point; rather, Berke Khan's conversion was a pivotal moment that led to increased Islamic influence among the Mongols, especially in Eastern Europe, parts of Russia, and the northwestern region of Central Asia.[57]

# Berke Takes Charge of
# the Golden Horde

*"God has promised those of you who believe and do good that He will certainly make them successors in the land, as He did with those before them; and will surely establish for them their faith which He has chosen for them; and will indeed change their fear into security—'provided that' they worship Me, associating nothing with Me."* – Qur'an 24:55

After Möngke Khan's death in 1259, the Mongol Empire divided into four major khanates: the Yuan Dynasty (Mongol Empire in China), the Ilkhanate (in Iran and surrounding regions), the Chagatai Khanate (in parts of Central Asia and eventually southern parts of modern Kazakhstan and parts of Xinjiang, China), and the Golden Horde.[58] The divide was due to a combination of succession disputes, internal strife, vast geographical distances, and administrative challenges.[59] The lack of a clear line of succession led to rival claims to the throne, exacerbating tensions among Mongol leaders. The immense size of the empire made centralized governance challenging, encouraging regional leaders to assert greater autonomy. These factors, alongside varying local cultures and economies within the empire's territories, contributed to the formal division into the four aforementioned khanates, each ruled by different branches of Genghis Khan's descendants.[60]

As already stated, the original Khan of the Golden Horde region was Batu Khan (the son of Jochi), a grandson of Genghis Khan. Batu Khan established the Golden Horde, also known as the Kipchak Khanate, in the mid-13th century and expanded its territory into parts of Eastern Europe and Russia. After Batu's death in 1255, his succession was followed by a series of leaders from his lineage: the short reigns of Sartak and Ulaghchi (Ulakçı). Afterward, the next notable khan to come to power was Berke Khan, Batu's brother, who is recognized as the fourth khan of the Golden Horde.[61] In addition to being the first Mongol Muslim leader, Berke is also known for his significant role in the Mongol civil wars, particularly against the Ilkhanate. He was also the first khan to be selected exclusively by the Jochids without the endorsement of the Great Khan. He ruled the Golden Horde from around 1257 until his death in 1266.[62]

## His Leadership and Alliances

*"Cooperate with one another in goodness and righteousness, and do not cooperate in sin and transgression. And be mindful of God."* – Qur'an 5:2

It is often reported that Berke proved very skillful at stabilizing the Golden Horde, the Mongol Empire's western section. Under his leadership, for instance, the Horde needed to establish new methods for economic stability and political power. This would give them leverage to create an autonomous entity separate from the Great Khan and resist pressure from other Mongol groups, particularly the Ilkhanids. Although the Jochids were nearly strangled by Toluid pressure and embargos after Hülegü sought to take over the Middle East (territories under the domain of the Jochids), the Horde survived such pressures due in part to Berke's economic alliances with the Mamluks, the Genoese and the Byzantines.[63]

Under Berke's rule, the Mongols quashed Danylo of Halych's revolt[a] and launched a second assault on Poland and Lithuania

---

[a] Danylo of Halych's revolt against the Mongols was a significant event in the mid-13th century. Danylo Romanovych, also known as Daniel of Galicia, was the ruler of the Kingdom of Galicia-

in 1259, led by General Burundai. A raid on Bulgaria and Byzantine Thrace followed in 1265. Subsequently, Michael VIII Palaiologos of the Byzantine Empire was left with no choice but to send valuable fabrics and other goods to the Golden Horde as tribute.[64]

At home, Berke was a highly respected leader among Muslims and the non-Muslim Mongols within his domain even before his khanship. William of Rubruck, a Franciscan missionary and explorer, for instance, noted very early on that although Berke did not allow pork to be consumed within his camp, he was very tolerant of Christians and other religious communities.[a] In his accounts, Rubruck mentioned that Berke allowed freedom of worship within his domain and interacted amicably with various religious groups, reflecting his relatively inclusive and diplomatic approach to governance.[b]

---

Volhynia, located in modern-day Ukraine. For details, see May and Hope, eds., *The Mongol World*, 2022.

[a] In another instance, the Venetian brothers Niccolò and Maffeo Polo (the father and uncle of Marco Polo) left their homeland seeking business opportunities and eventually reached the court of Berke Khan in Saray. There, Berke granted them permission to trade in the markets, and it is said that the brothers profited greatly during their year-long stay. See Harl, *Empires of the Steppes*, 379, 2023.

[b] William of Rubruck is said to have spent significant time with Möngke Khan from 1253 to 1255 during his mission to the Mongol court. He visited the court in Karakorum, where he had several audiences with the khan, documenting his observations and experiences in his detailed report, which provides valuable insights into Mongol culture and the inner workings of the Mongol Empire during the mid-13th century. For details, see Jackson, translator, *The Mission of Friar William of Rubruck*, 2009.

The diplomatic relationships Berke built with outside powers were very beneficial to his people and the geopolitics of the region at large. The documentation of interactions between the Horde and the Mamluk Sultanate, for instance, offers particular insights. Over two centuries, these superpowers engaged in a significant number of communications, with over eighty diplomatic missions recorded. The correspondence exchanged between khans, sultans, and their envoys—accessible through Arabic texts—illuminates the political and military matters of the time even after the death of Berke Khan.[65]

As for the relationship between Berke and the Mamluks, there is no definite date for when it first began, but we know for certain that it was solidified between 1260 and 1262. Following the Mongol defeat in Palestine by the outnumbered Mamluks at 'Ain Jalut in 1260, Berke saw an opportunity to counter the growing power of the Ilkhanate led by Hülegü Khan.[66] Recognizing the strategic advantage, Berke formed an alliance with the Mamluks, the powerful rulers of Egypt. Initially, he allied with Sultan Qutuz (r. 1259–1260), who was instrumental in the Mamluk victory at 'Ain Jalut. Following the assassination of Qutuz, Berke maintained the alliance with his successor, Sultan Baybars (r. 1260–1277). Baybars, as he was known by his Kipchak surname, was the fourth Sultan of the Mamluk state in Egypt, and he is said to have ushered in an era of unmatched prosperity in the region.[67]

This alliance proved mutually beneficial. For the Mamluks, it provided crucial support against the Ilkhanate's attempts to expand into the Levant and Egypt. (It is said that Baybars had Berke's name announced after his own in Mecca, Medinah, and

Jerusalem; an act demonstrating Baybars' respect for the Khan of the Golden Horde while also asserting his own influence over the Islamic holy cities, which reinforced his claim as leader of the *ummah*).[68] For the Golden Horde, it offered a chance to weaken Hülegü's forces and to gain an influential ally in the region, in addition to economic advantages. This collaboration included coordinated military actions and exchanges of envoys, cementing a partnership that significantly influenced the political landscape of the Middle East and the region during the late 13th century.[69]

# The Fall of Baghdad and the Mongol Divide

*"... Whoever takes a life—unless as a punishment for murder or mischief in the land—it will be as if they killed all of humanity; and whoever saves a life, it will be as if they saved all of humanity."*
– Qur'an 5:32

By 1219, the Mongol Empire had launched its conquest of Muslim lands. In 1225, Genghis Khan's armies decimated the Khwarezm-Shah state and took over northern Iran.[70] The Abbasid armies under Caliph al-Mustansir (r. 1226–1242) repelled a Mongol assault on Arabian Iraq, and his successor, al-Mustasim (r. 1242–1258), withstood a Mongol siege in 1245, but successive floods from 1243 to 1256 greatly weakened Baghdad's defenses, economy, and morale. In 1258, Hülegü managed to capture Baghdad, leading to al-Mustasim's execution.[71] The fall of the magnificent city and the execution of the caliph marked the end of an era of Muslim civilization; the universally recognized caliphate came to an abrupt and violent end, thus severely impacting global Muslim leadership. Baghdad was largely destroyed, with an estimated 800,000 to over a million casualties.[72]

Ibn Katheer, the esteemed Muslim historian, described the terrible events as follows:

> They [the Mongols] attacked the country and killed everyone they found of the men, women, children and elderly. Many people hid in wells, rubbish bins and grasslands for days; while others grouped together and locked themselves inside shops and mosques, but the Tatars broke in, by demolishing the doors or burning the fronts, and once inside, they chased the fleeing residents; slaughtering them on the roofs. None escaped from the massacre, except for Jews, Christians and those who had sought their protection.[73]

After the devastation, the then-center of the Muslim world with all its cultural heritage and knowledge was now reduced to rubble and turned into a province under Mongol rule.[74] The news of this loss sparked outrage across the Muslim world, and even among the Mongol leadership itself. This included Berke Khan, who was left with no choice but to oppose his cousin, Hülegü.[75]

Berke had also taken personal offense that Hülegü had never consulted him regarding his ruthless actions in Baghdad.[76] It is reported that Berke said the following to his Mongol community after receiving the news of the destruction of Baghdad: "He (Hülegü) has sacked all the cities of the Muslims, and has brought about the death of the Caliph. With the help of God, I will call him to account for so much innocent blood."[77]

As for Hülegü, he was set to continue his conquests across the Muslim world and the region, including Egypt,

Syria, and possibly the holy cities of Mecca, Medinah, and Jerusalem.[78] However, news of the Great Khan's death in Karakorum, the Mongol Empire's center, forced him to delay his campaign and return to Mongolia to resolve succession issues.[79] After addressing these issues at home, Hülegü resumed his efforts to conquer and dominate the remaining Muslim territories, but this time he faced resistance from the inside.[80]

# The Civil War of 1261–1262

*"Fight against them ⸢if they persecute you⸣ until there is no more persecution, and ⸢your⸣ devotion will be to God ⸢alone⸣. If they stop ⸢persecuting you⸣, let there be no hostility except against the aggressors."* – Qur'an 2:193

Until 1256, the two Mongol powers had acted together in the name of the Great Khan, but competition and conflict arose when Hülegü and Berke Khan could not peacefully resolve their differences. For decades, Hülegü himself had gradually encroached on the Horde's territories, seizing lands that Genghis Khan had designated for the Jochids.[81] During the Ilkhanate's invasion of present-day Azerbaijan (another chunk of land Genghis Khan had granted to his son Jochi), they harassed and killed merchants from the Golden Horde in their own territory.[82] Instances like these, as well as the reluctance of the Ilkhanids to share tax revenues from eastern Iran, led to great discord between the two Mongol leaders.[83]

By this time, Berke had already been in contact with the Mamluks, proposing a joint fight against Hülegü, who was now invading Muslim countries and oppressing their people. Berke had also promised the Mamluk sultan to give back all the Muslim lands that Hülegü had conquered.[84] The only way forward, at this point, became full-scale warfare.

The civil war between the Golden Horde and the Ilkhanate was a significant conflict within the Mongol Empire, illustrating the internal divisions that began to emerge among the different Mongol khanates and/or their rulers.[85] It is now well known that Berke Khan went against Hülegü Khan, the ruler of the Ilkhanate, primarily due to ideological and religious differences, as well as family grievances and territorial disputes.[86] As a Muslim, Berke Khan, as well as his Muslim allies, were enraged by Hülegü's destruction of Baghdad and the Abbasid Caliphate in 1258. The Toluids, led by Hülegü, supported the Christian communities, especially in the Middle East.[87] This religious discord was compounded by Hülegü's claims over territories in the Caucasus, which both khans sought to control, but were in fact under the domain of the Jochids since the death of Genghis Khan.[88]

In 1262, the conflict escalated to war. Hülegü Khan faced a significant loss during his invasion attempts north of the Caucasus. At the Battle of the Terek River, Hülegü's forces were ambushed by Berke's troops led by General Nogai, a nephew of Berke. Hülegü's army suffered a major defeat, with many soldiers either killed or drowned as the river's ice broke beneath them. Following this loss, Hülegü was left with no choice but to withdraw his forces back to present-day Azerbaijan.[89] The conflict marked one of the first major internal wars within the Mongol Empire and highlighted the growing fractures among the Mongol khanates.[90]

During the war, Berke had the additional advantage of a military ally in the region. As previously noted, Berke supported the Mamluks of Egypt and Syria due to his alliance with Sultan Baybars, who himself hoped to restore the Abbasid Caliphate in Baghdad after its devastation by Hülegü's forces.[91] In an attempt to face and repel a common threat, Berke's armies marched south of the Golden Horde to end Hülegü's advancements, but after a number of skirmishes with Hülegü's armies in the Caucasus and pressure from Kublai Khan, Berke withdrew his troops from the region.[92] The civil war ended without a decisive victory, but it set the stage for further divisions and conflicts among the Mongol successor states.[93]

## His Life and Death

*"Every soul will taste death. And you will only receive your full reward on the Day of Judgment. Whoever is spared from the Fire and is admitted into Paradise will ˹indeed˺ triumph, whereas the life of this world is no more than the delusion of enjoyment."*
– Qur'an 3:185

Berke significantly shaped the Horde, becoming the first khan chosen solely by the Jochids without the Great Khan's approval, marking a move towards independence from the Toluid-led Mongol core.[94] He shifted the Horde towards Islam, significantly changing its culture, politics, and international relations, especially with Muslim communities. When nomadic leaders embraced Islam, the court of the khan emerged as a significant center in the Islamic world, a fact that is often overlooked in Islamic history. We now know that itinerant scholars and artisans from places like Anatolia, Central Asia, Egypt, and Syria found hospitality in the Jochi Ulus.[95]

Despite these changes, Berke retained Mongol governance features like trade, vassalage, as well as tolerance for the diverse communities within the empire. Challenges, such as economic threats from the Ilkhanids, were overcome through alliances with the Mamluks and new trade connections in the region, showcasing Berke's ability to adapt Mongol traditions to new circumstances.[96]

Following Hülegü's death in 1265, his successor Abaqa Khan (r. 1256–1265) continued the same hostile policy against the Golden Horde. That same year, forces of the Ilkhanate and the Golden Horde faced each other near the Kura River (present-day Azerbaijan). The forces on both sides of the river waited in battle formation for days. Berke planned to cross the river towards Tbilisi (present-day Georgia) and then attack the Ilkhanate, but he fell ill and died in 1266 before he could carry out his plan.[97] No major health concerns were recorded, but Berke—like his brother Batu—reportedly suffered from gout.[98]

According to tradition, Berke's body was taken to the capital city, Saray, and buried there. Since he had no sons, Mengü Timur (Möngke-Temur), a grandson of Batu, was declared khan of the Golden Horde.[99] Mengü Timur maintained the alliance with the Mamluks while also continuing his efforts to contain the threats of the Ilkhanate.[100]

It is crucial to note too that, after Berke Khan's death in 1266, several of his successors diligently continued Berke's legacy, particularly in regard to strengthening the Golden Horde and solidifying Islam within its territories.[101] This transformation, however, wasn't immediate but gradually took place throughout the late 13th and into the 14th century. Some of those influential successors include Uzbeg or Özbek Khan (r. 1313–1341), Tïnïbeg (r. 1341–1342), Janibeg (r. 1342–1357), Berdibeg (r. 1357–1359), and others.[102]

# The Legacy of the Golden Horde

*"Perhaps you dislike something which is good for you and like something which is bad for you. God knows and you do not know."*
– Qur'an 2:216

As Favereau notes, by the mid-1260s, Jochid dominance over the western steppe was undisputed among the Mongols.[103] Even the Great Khan had to acknowledge that the Horde, a Mongol confederation, had become a unified power, comprising a diverse and integrated realm of Mongols, Russians, and Caucasians; pagans, Christians, and Muslims; city-dwellers and herders—a nomadic kingdom in its own right, thanks in part to the leadership of Berke.[104]

Generally speaking, the Golden Horde's influence in the region at large had deep consequences on the political, economic, religious, and cultural map of modern Eurasia. Scholars have shown the unique way in which Islam unified and socially integrated peoples, by shaping community life and collective memory and by respecting local culture within the framework of Islam. Because of this, for centuries the Horde continued to remain a broadly multi-ethnic and multi-religious khanate that always included various peoples and religions under Mongol rule.

Naturally, Islam did not spread overnight as local beliefs and traditions persisted in the region. Instead, it spread gradually among the Genghisid family and the broader Mongol populations, arguably taking over 150 years for the majority of the Genghisids and their military to convert. Moreover, Islamization likely wasn't achieved in any Genghisid or former Genghisid domains until at least the early 15th century.[105] Today, the former territories of the Golden Horde encompass present-day Russia, Ukraine, Kazakhstan, Kyrgyzstan, and Uzbekistan, the last three being Muslim-majority countries.[106]

The origin stories of the Tatars and other Central Eurasian communities extend back to the period when the khans Berke and Özbek converted to Islam.[107] Özbek Khan (r. 1313–1341), in this case, was another pivotal figure in the history of the Golden Horde due to his conversion to Islam and subsequent efforts to establish it as the dominant religion within his realm.[108] His conversion marked a significant shift, as it signaled the formal adoption of Islam by the Mongol elite in the region. Özbek Khan's embrace of Islam not only enhanced his legitimacy among the empire's Muslim subjects but also strengthened political and economic ties with neighboring Muslim states.[109] Under his rule, Islamic institutions flourished, with the establishment of mosques, *madrasa*s, and the promotion of Islamic law. Özbek Khan's reign thus solidified the integration of Muslim culture and religion within the Golden Horde, laying a foundation that influenced the region's religious and cultural landscape for centuries to come. His efforts ensured that Islam became deeply ingrained in the social and political fabric of the Golden Horde, enduring long after his reign.[110] Because of this, many Muslims now living in the

Russian Federation see this timeframe as a formative period in their history. Indeed, as it has often been noted, Islamization is one of the Golden Horde's most important legacies.[111]

The Golden Horde's land holdings were the greatest in the 13th century when it controlled a large area encompassing Russia, Ukraine, Kazakhstan, and the Caucasus. Its dominance lasted until the 15th century, and it was also one of the longest-lasting Mongol khanates. Although the Golden Horde began to fragment in the late 14th century, remnants of it, particularly the Khanate of Crimea, persisted into the 18th century. The Crimean Khanate, a successor state of the Golden Horde, became a vassal of the Ottoman Empire and survived until it was annexed by the Russian Empire in 1783.[112]

Yet, overall, the impact of the Mongol Empire on the region's history and culture has largely been overlooked. Only recently, historians, archaeologists, and philologists have begun to significantly illuminate this crucial era of Mongol influence in the former Golden Horde territories.[113]

When considering the legacy of empires, notes Favereau, we acknowledge the cosmopolitan impact of Mediterranean, European, and Ottoman powers, which connected the world through tolerance, coercion, exploration, protection, investment, and conquest. These empires are often credited with shaping global history. However, nomadic societies also significantly influenced global history, and the Horde is a testament to that influence and transformation.[114]

# The Legacy of Berke Khan

*"We ˹also˺ made them leaders, guiding by Our command, and inspired them to do good deeds, establish prayer, and pay alms-tax. And they were devoted to Our worship." –* Qur'an 21:73

Long after Berke passed away in 1266, his legacy continues to inspire Muslims and many non-Muslims across the globe. Here are just a few points on how Berke is remembered and his legacy lives on:

1. Some historians believe that Berke's actions against Hülegü (and the Great Khan) helped protect the Holy Lands—Mecca, Medinah, and Jerusalem—from suffering the same destruction that befell Baghdad.

2. Like many of his predecessors, Berke was very tolerant of people of different faiths.

3. Although Berke became a sultan in the Muslim world, he continued to serve as a khan in his domain, committed to his faith, cause and community.[115]

4. According to the writings of Juzjani and al-Juwayni, Berke applied both *yasa* (Mongol law) with non-Muslims, and *shariah* with Muslims, remaining sincerely committed to the spirit of both systems in the context of his khanate.[116]

5. Berke established schools for teaching the Qur'an, maintained imams and muezzins in Saray, and protected the scholars, no matter their religious affiliations.[117]

6. Under Berke Khan, the Golden Horde experienced its most glorious era, becoming fully independent from the Great Khanate of the old Mongol Empire.[118]

7. His diplomatic and military actions helped maintain the Silk Road as a safe route for trade between the East and the West, bolstering economic stability and cultural exchange. Commercial relations with Turkestan, for instance, increased, leading to the rapid spread of Islam there.

8. Berke struck his own coins (ca. 1263–1267) which contained Arabic inscriptions with Islamic references.

9. Although not all Jochids became Muslim, due to Berke's influential example and his short but successful leadership, Islam spread and continues to thrive in the lands of the former Golden Horde to this day.[119]

10. Because Islam was firmly established in the Golden Horde due to Berke's and his Muslim successors' influence in the region, after 1330 Christian missionary work into the Golden Horde mostly ceased,[120] although existing Christian and Buddhist communities continued to thrive there.

# Glossary[a]

| | |
|---|---|
| ﷺ: | lit. 'peace and blessings of God be upon him' |
| **Altan orugh:** | 'Golden family'; the imperial Mongol dynasty |
| **Amir al-umara:** | Chief amir; high-ranking military commander |
| **Bakhshi:** | Buddhist monk associated with the Mongol court |
| **Basqaq:** | Intendant or governor responsible for administration; regional administrator |
| **Beglerbegi:** | High-ranking official or chief amir |
| **Bichechi:** | Scribe or secretary; recorder of official documents; also *bitikchi* |
| **Cumans/Kumans:** | A Turkic nomadic people from Central Asia |
| **Darughachi:** | Governor; official in charge of a specific region |
| **Dhimmi:** | Non-Muslims (Jews, Christians) living under Muslim rule |
| **Elchi:** | Envoy or courier; person sent on diplomatic missions |
| **Faqir:** | Ascetic; individual devoted to spiritual life |
| **Ili/El:** | Peace or submission; term for political stability |
| **Ilkhanate** | lit. 'subordinate khanate' |

---

[a] Although not individually indicated, many of the terms here have either Arabic, Turkic, Persian or Mongol origins.

**Iqta:** Land grant or revenue assignment given to military officers

**Jizya:** Tax levied on non-Muslims in Islamic states

**Keshig:** Guard corps; elite unit protecting the ruler

**Khan:** Monarch or military leader. Title given to a ruler or military leader in various Central Asian, Middle Eastern, and Mongol cultures, historically signifying authority and leadership over a tribe, clan, or empire

**Khanate:** Empire in the context of 13th century Mongolia

**Khatun:** Queen or princess; female royalty

**Khutba:** Sermon delivered during Friday prayers

**Küregen:** Royal son-in-law; married into the ruling family

**Madrasa:** School; religious seminary

**Möchelge:** Written pledge or agreement

**Na'ib:** Deputy or viceroy; someone who governs in absence of the ruler

**Nökör:** Comrade or associate; term for a loyal companion

**Noyan:** Military commander; leader of Mongol troops

**Oghul:** Prince of the blood; member of the royal family

**Ordo/Orda:** Camp or headquarters; main settlement of the khan

**Ortaq:** Business partner; especially in trade agreements with Mongols

**Qaghan:** Emperor; supreme ruler of the Mongols

**Qol/Qul:** Central area or core, especially in military or property contexts

**Qubchur:** Head tax initially levied on nomads, later extended to settled populations

**Quriltai/kuriltai:** Assembly or gathering, often for political or military decisions

**Shah:** King or ruler

**Shariah:** Islamic code of law; way of life

**Shihna:** Governor or official representative

**Tenggeri:** Heaven or sky; divine element in Mongol spirituality

**Tümen:** Unit of 10,000 soldiers; also used to denote a large quantity of money

**Ulama:** Scholars or learned individuals in Islamic contexts

**Ulus:** Appanage; gifted territory or domain ruled by a Mongol prince, including peoples and lands

**Ummah:** The global community of Muslims, united by their shared faith in Islam

**Waqf:** Religious endowment for charity, typically in Islamic law

**Wazir:** Chief minister or advisor to the ruler

**Yam:** Courier relay network; system for official communications

**Yarghu:** Court of inquiry; judicial assembly

**Yasa:** Law or regulation; part of the Mongol legal system

**Yurt:** Nomadic encampment or area used for pasture

**Zakat:** Obligatory almsgiving in Islam, one of the five pillars

# Appendix A

## Timeline of the Mongol Empire and Islam (1206–1405)

**1206:** Temüjin is proclaimed Genghis Khan, uniting the Mongol tribes and beginning the Mongol Empire

**1207–1227:** Mongol conquests in Northeast Asia

**1218:** Genghis Khan sends a trade mission to the Khwarezmian Empire; the trade delegates are executed, leading to the Mongol invasion

**1219–1221:** Mongol invasion of the Khwarezmian Empire, resulting in the destruction of major cities like Bukhara and Samarkand

**1227:** Genghis Khan dies; Ögedei Khan becomes the Great Khan

**1235–1241:** Mongol invasions of Europe and the Middle East, including the destruction of Baghdad in 1258

**1237–1240:** Mongol invasion of Kievan Rus'

**1241:** Ögedei Khan dies; Güyük Khan is elected the Great Khan five years later

**1246–1248:** Reign of Güyük Khan, including continued expansion into the Middle East and Europe

**1251:** Möngke Khan becomes the Great Khan

**1253–1258:** Hülegü Khan's campaigns in the Middle East, leading to the fall of Baghdad

**1257:** Berke Khan becomes the ruler of the Golden Horde

**1259:** Following the death of Möngke Khan, by the mid-1260s the Mongol Empire is divided into four khanates

**1260:** Battle of 'Ain Jalut, where the Mamluks defeat the Mongols, halting their advance into Egypt

**1262:** Berke-Hülegü war, a conflict between the Golden Horde and the Ilkhanate over religious and territorial disputes

**1295:** Ghazan Khan converts to Islam and becomes ruler of the Ilkhanate, promoting Islam within his territories

**1295–1304:** Ilkhanate's conquests in the Middle East

**1313–1341:** Reign of Özbek Khan, marked by the further Islamization of the Golden Horde and political stability
**1335–1350s:** The decline of the Ilkhans

**1368:** Ming Dynasty overthrows the Mongols in China

**1360s–1405:** Decline and dissolution of the Mongol Empire

# Appendix B

## The Great Khans (and the Regents)
## of the Mongol Empire

**1206–1227**  Temüjin (Genghis Khan)
**1227–1229**  Tolui, Regent
**1229–1241**  Ögedei Khan
**1242–1246**  Töregene, Regent
**1246–1248**  Güyük Khan
**1248–1251**  Oghul-Qaimish, Regent
**1251–1259**  Möngke Khan

# Appendix C

## Khans of the Golden Horde

| | |
|---|---|
| d. **1227** | Jochi Khan (son of Genghis Khan) |
| **1227–1255** | Batu Khan (son of Jochi) |
| **1256–1257** | Sartaq Khan |
| **1256–1257** | Ulaghchi Khan |
| **1257–1266** | Berke Khan |
| **1267–1280** | Mengü-Temür Khan |
| **1280–1287** | Töde-Mengü Khan |
| **1287–1291** | Töle-Bugha Khan |
| **1291–1312** | Toqto'a Khan |
| **1313–1341** | Özbek Khan |
| **1341–1342** | Tïnïbeg Khan |
| **1342–1357** | Janibeg Khan |
| **1357–1359** | Berdibeg Khan |
| **1359–1360** | Qulpa Khan |
| **1360** | Nawroz Khan[121] |

# Appendix D

## Depiction of the Battle of the Terek River in 1262

**Fig 1.** Battle at the Terek, 1262. Hayton of Corycus,
*Fleur des histoires d'Orient.*[a]

---

[a] The painting is said to have been completed in the early 14th century.
Public domain from Wikimedia Commons, accessed in 2024.

# Endnotes

**1**     These symbols are used in standardized transliteration systems such as the ISO 233, DIN 31635, or the Buckwalter transliteration system, among others.

**2**     " ' " represents the Arabic letter ع ('ayn), which is a voiced pharyngeal fricative, a sound that doesn't have a direct equivalent in the Latin alphabet. The character " ' " is called a "turned comma" or "ayn" in transliteration systems.

**3**     For details, see Rahman, *A Chronology Of Islamic History*, 1-3, 1989.

**4**     'sic' is often used to denote an error in the original or acknowledge that a term or phrase used in the original is no longer appropriate in current times.

**5**     All Qur'an translations in this book are from Khattab, translator, *The Clear Quran*, 2015.

6     See De Hartog, *Genghis Khan*, 165, 2004; Favereau, *The Horde*, 127, 2021.

**7**     After the Mongol conquest, Russian chroniclers referred to the nomads of the Jochid Ulus collectively as "Tatars" and often called the Jochid Ulus the "Horde." See Roman Hautala in May and Hope, eds., *The Mongol World*, 247, 2022.

**8**     See Benjamin, *The Mongol Empire*, 2021; Prawdin, *The Mongol Empire*, 2005. See also Galstyan, *Ermeni Kaynaklarına Göre Moğollar*, 2018.

**9** Atwood, *Encyclopedia of Mongolia and the Mongol Empire*, 202, 2004; Nicolle, T*he Mongol Warlords*, 118. See also Philipp and Haarmann, eds., *The Mamluks in Egyptian Politics and Society*, 2007.

**10** See Rossabi, *Khubilai Khan*, 54, 1988; Weatherford, *Genghis Khan and the Making of the Modern World*, 189-190, 2004. See also De Nicola, "The Queen of the Chaghatayids," vol. 26, no. 1/2, 112, 2016.

**11** See De Nicola, "The Queen of the Chaghatayids," vol. 26, no. 1/2, 112, 2016; Favereau, *The Horde*, 146, 2021.

**12** See, for instance, Omar of the Orient, "How the sons of Genghis Khan converted the Mongols to Islam," 2023; Benjamin, *The Mongol Empire*, 2021.

**13** See, for instance, Weatherford, *Genghis Khan and the Making of the Modern World*, 289, 2004.

**14** Kublai Khan was a descendant of the Tolui lineage of the Mongol Empire. Tolui was the youngest son of Genghis Khan. See Rossabi, *Khubilai Khan*, 1988.

**15** See Weatherford, *Genghis Khan and the Making of the Modern World*, 289, 2004; Benjamin, *The Mongol Empire*, 2021. See also Atwood, *Encyclopedia of Mongolia and the Mongol Empire*, 2004.

**16** Hadith in *Sahih al-Bukhari*.

**17** As some historians have noted, Jochi's lineage was often questioned regarding whether he really was Genghis Khan's son, but the Khan still accepted Jochi as part of his family. See, for instance, Benjamin, *The Mongol Empire*, 2021.

**18** Roman Hautala in May and Hope, eds., *The Mongol World*, 245, 2022. See also Favereau, *The Horde*, 2021.

**19** Broadbridge, *Women and the Making of the Mongol Empire*, 231–232, 2018; Howorth, *History of the Mongols* (II), 103, 1880; Favereau, *The Horde*, 19, 2021.

**20** Cf. Howorth, *History of the Mongols* (II), 103-104, 1880.

**21** Favereau, *The Horde*, 102, 2021.

**22**     Jackson, *The Mongols and the Islamic World*, 348, 2017. See also Juzjani, *Tabakât-i-Nasirî*, 1970.

**23**     DeWeese, *Islamization and Native Religion in the Golden Horde*, 86, 2010.

**24**     Halperin, *Russian and Mongols*, 336, 2007; Konukçu, "Berke Han" in İslâm Ansiklopedisi, 506-507. See also Kaya, translator, *Moğolların Gizli Tarihçesi*, 2018.

**25**     See Ölmez, "On Mongolian asara- 'to nourish' and Turkish aşa…" 242, 2007; Konukçu, "Berke Han" in İslâm Ansiklopedisi, 506.

**26**     Hadith in *Sunan Abu Dawud*.

**27**     Weatherford, *Genghis Khan and the Making of the Modern World*, 143-145, 2004; Wolfe, *Batu, Khan of the Golden Horde*, 2020.

**28**     De Hartog, *Genghis Khan*, 167-168, 2004. See also Harl, *Empires of the Steppes*, 319-329, 2023.

**29**     Atwood, *Encyclopedia of Mongolia and the Mongol Empire*, 202, 2004; Jackson, *The Mongols and the Islamic World*, 144, 2017. See also De Hartog, *Genghis Khan*, 165, 2004.

**30**     Vásáry, "'History and Legend' in Berke Khan's Conversion to Islam," 235-236, 1990; DeWeese, *Islamization and Native Religion in the Golden Horde*, 84, 2010.

**31**     Cf. Favereau, *The Horde*, 141, 2021. See also Benjamin, *The Mongol Empire*, 2021; DeWeese, *Islamization and Native Religion in the Golden Horde*, 2010.

**32**     See Konukçu, "Berke Han" in İslâm Ansiklopedisi, 506.

**33**     See Hundley, *The Mongol Empire in World History*, 9, 2017. See also Morgan, *The Mongols*, 2007; Benjamin, *The Mongol Empire*, 2021; Galstyan, *Ermeni Kaynaklarına Göre Moğollar*, 2018.

**34**     See Frashëri, *Himmat al-himam fiy nashr al-Islam*, 1885; Jackson, *The Mongols and the Islamic World*, 2017; Arnold, *The Preaching of Islam*, 2018.

**35**     See Benjamin, *The Mongol Empire*, 2021; Arnold, *The*

*Preaching of Islam*, 2018; Frashëri, *Himmat al-himam fiy nashr al-Islam*, 1885.

**36**     DeWeese, *Islamization and Native Religion in the Golden Horde*, 84, 2010.

**37**     Vásáry, "'History and Legend' in Berke Khan's Conversion to Islam," 241, 1990; Halperin, *Russian and Mongols*, 16, 2007.

**38**     Favereau, *The Horde*, 138-140, 2021; Atwood, *Encyclopedia of Mongolia and the Mongol Empire*, 73, 2004.

**39**     See Philipp and Haarmann, eds., *The Mamluks in Egyptian Politics and Society*, 2007; Favereau, *The Horde*, 2021. See also Galstyan, *Ermeni Kaynaklarına Göre Moğollar*, 2018.

**40**     Vásáry, "'History and Legend' in Berke Khan's Conversion to Islam," 235, 1990.

**41**     DeWeese, *Islamization and Native Religion in the Golden Horde*, 83-84, 2010. See also Favereau, *The Horde*, 141, 2021; Ishayahu Landa in May and Hope, eds., *The Mongol World*, 647, 2022.

**42**     Vásáry, "'History and Legend' in Berke Khan's Conversion to Islam," 235-236, 1990; Favereau, *The Horde*, 159, 2021.

**43**     Harl, *Empires of the Steppes*, 331, 2023. See also Omar of the Orient, "How the sons of Genghis Khan converted the Mongols to Islam," 2023; Vásáry, "'History and Legend' in Berke Khan's Conversion to Islam," 232-252, 1990.

**44**     See, for instance, Vásáry, "'History and Legend' in Berke Khan's Conversion to Islam," 232-252, 1990; Konukçu, "Berke Han" in İslâm Ansiklopedisi, 506-507.

**45**     Jackson, *The Mongols and the Islamic World*, 345, 2017; Vásáry, "'History and Legend' in Berke Khan's Conversion to Islam," 239, 1990.

**46**     Uludağ, "Seyfeddin Bâharzî," in İslâm Ansiklopedisi, 474-475; Vásáry, "'History and Legend' in Berke Khan's Conversion to Islam," 239, 1990.

**47**     DeWeese, *Islamization and Native Religion in the Golden Horde*, 83-84, 2010; Vásáry, "'History and Legend' in Berke Khan's

Conversion to Islam," 247-248, 1990; Favereau, *The Horde*, 159, 2021.

**48**      This event is also often cited as, "around the late 1250s to early 1260s." See Harl, *Empires of the Steppes*, 331, 2023.

**49**      Abu al-Ghazi is known for his magnum opus called Shajara-i Turk. See *DeWeese, Islamization and Native Religion in the Golden Horde*, 199, 366, 2010.

**50**      Vásáry, "'History and Legend' in Berke Khan's Conversion to Islam," 241, 1990; DeWeese, *Islamization and Native Religion in the Golden Horde*, 86, 2010.

**51**      DeWeese, *Islamization and Native Religion in the Golden Horde*, 84, 2010; Vásáry, "'History and Legend' in Berke Khan's Conversion to Islam," 251, 1990.

**52**      Jackson, *The Mongols and the Islamic World*, 348, 2017; Vásáry, "'History and Legend' in Berke Khan's Conversion to Islam," 249-250, 1990; Favereau, *The Horde*, 160, 2021.

**53**      DeWeese, *Islamization and Native Religion in the Golden Horde*, 84, 2010; Vásáry, "'History and Legend' in Berke Khan's Conversion to Islam," 250, 1990.

**54**      DeWeese, *Islamization and Native Religion in the Golden Horde*, 84-85, 2010.

**55**      Favereau, *The Horde*, 19, 2021; Atwood, *Encyclopedia of Mongolia and the Mongol Empire*, 73, 2004.

**56**      Vásáry, "Orthodox Christian Qumans and Tatars of the Crimea in the 13th - 14th centuries," 271, 1988. See also Favereau-Doumenjou, "New Collective Monograph," 921, 2016; DeWeese, *Islamization and Native Religion in the Golden Horde*, 2010; Halperin, *Russia and the Golden Horde*, 1987.

**57**      See Favereau-Doumenjou, "New Collective Monograph," 921, 2016. See also DeWeese, *Islamization and Native Religion in the Golden Horde*, 2010; Halperin, *Russia and the Golden Horde*, 1987; See also Galstyan, *Ermeni Kaynaklarına Göre Moğollar*, 2018.

**58**      Jackson, *The Mongols and the Islamic World*, 182, 2017.

See Hundley, *The Mongol Empire in World History*, 2017; Jackson, *The Mongols and the West*, 2018.

**59**     See De Nicola, "The Queen of the Chaghatayids," vol. 26, no. 1/2, 112, 2016. See also Weatherford, *Genghis Khan and the Making of the Modern World*, 2004.

**60**     See Benjamin, *The Mongol Empire*, 2021; Jackson, *The Mongols and the West*, 2018; Prawdin, *The Mongol Empire*, 2005.

**61**     Jackson, *The Mongols and the Islamic World*, 122, 2017. See also DeWeese, *Islamization and Native Religion in the Golden Horde*, 2010.

**62**     Vásáry, "'History and Legend' in Berke Khan's Conversion to Islam," 245, 1990. See also Benjamin, *The Mongol Empire*, 2021; DeWeese, *Islamization and Native Religion in the Golden Horde*, 2010.

**63**     Favereau, *The Horde*, 149, 2021. See also Konukçu, "Berke Han" in İslâm Ansiklopedisi, 506-507.

**64**     Konukçu, "Berke Han" in İslâm Ansiklopedisi, 506-507. See also Morgan, *The Mongols*, 2007.

**65**     Favereau, *The Horde*, 24, 2021. See also DeWeese, *Islamization and Native Religion in the Golden Horde*, 2010; Philipp and Haarmann, eds., *The Mamluks in Egyptian Politics and Society*, 2007.

**66**     Dupuy & Dupuy, *The Harper Encyclopedia of Military History*, 424, 1993. For more on 'Ain Jalut, Rossabi, *Khubilai Khan*, 54-56, 1988.

**67**     See Aigle, *The Mongol Empire Between Myth and Reality*, 224-225, 2014. See also Morgan, *The Mongols*, 2007; Philipp and Haarmann, eds., *The Mamluks in Egyptian Politics and Society*, 2007.

**68**     Aigle, *The Mongol Empire Between Myth and Reality*, 225, 2014.

**69**     Favereau, *The Horde*, 24, 2021. See also DeWeese, *Islamization and Native Religion in the Golden Horde*, 2010; Morgan, *The Mongols*, 2007; Philipp and Haarmann, eds., *The Mamluks in*

*Egyptian Politics and Society*, 2007.

**70**     For context, see May, *The Mongol Empire*, 2018; Morgan, *The Mongols*, 2007; Morton, *The Mongol Storm*, 2022.

**71**     Weatherford, *Genghis Khan and the Making of the Modern World*, 180-185, 2004. For details, see Benjamin, *The Mongol Empire*, 2021; Kaya, translator, *Moğolların Gizli Tarihçesi*, 2018.

**72**     See Frazier, "Invaders: Destroying Baghdad," 2005. For details, see Harl, *Empires of the Steppes*, 331-342, 2023.

**73**     As qtd. in Al-Salaabi, *Sultan Muhammad Al-Fatih*, 27, 2008. See also Benjamin, *The Mongol Empire*, 2021; Prawdin, *The Mongol Empire*, 2005.

**74**     See Hundley, *The Mongol Empire in World History*, 44-48, 2017. See also Lyons, *The House of Wisdom*, 2008.

**75**     DeWeese, *Islamization and Native Religion in the Golden Horde*, 84, 2010. See also Weatherford, *Genghis Khan and the Making of the Modern World*, 180-185, 2004; Vásáry, "'History and Legend' in Berke Khan's Conversion to Islam," 245, 1990.

**76**     Favereau, *The Horde*, 143, 2021.

**77**     See Nicolle, *The Mongol Warlords*, 119, 1998, citing Rashid al-Din's documentation of the statement by Berke Khan. The same quote is also found in *The Mamluk-Ilkhanid War* by Amitai-Preiss, 2005.

**78**     See Rashiduddin, *Jami u't-tawarikh: Compendium of Chronicles: A History of the Mongols*, (I), 1998; Morgan, *The Mongols*, 2007; Prawdin, *The Mongol Empire*, 2005.

**79**     Rossabi, *Khubilai Khan*, 54, 1988. See also May, *The Mongol Empire*, 2018; Morgan, *The Mongols*, 2007; Morton, *The Mongol Storm*, 2022.

**80**     Konukçu, "Berke Han" in İslâm Ansiklopedisi, 506-507; DeWeese, *Islamization and Native Religion in the Golden Horde*, 84, 2010. See also Weatherford, *Genghis Khan and the Making of the Modern World*, 180-185, 2004; Vásáry, "'History and Legend' in Berke Khan's Conversion to Islam," 245, 1990.

**81**     Favereau, *The Horde*, 146, 2021.

**82** Jackson, *The Mongols and the Islamic World*, 143, 2017. See also Rossabi, *The Mongols*, 2012.

**83** Favereau, *The Horde*, 146, 2021; Hundley, *The Mongol Empire in World History*, 54, 2017. See also Halperin, *Russia and the Golden Horde*, 1987.

**84** See Konukçu, "Berke Han" in İslâm Ansiklopedisi, 506-507; Rossabi, *The Mongols*, 87, 2012.

**85** See Benjamin, *The Mongol Empire*, 2021. See also Weatherford, *Genghis Khan and the Making of the Modern World*, 289, 2004.

**86** Nicolle, *The Mongol Warlords*, 118, 1998; Dupuy & Dupuy, T*he Harper Encyclopedia of Military History*, 422-424, 1993. See also Halperin, *Russia and the Golden Horde*, 1987.

**87** Although Hülegü was a shamanist, it is said that two of his wives were Nestorian Christian. See Harl, *Empires of the Steppes*, 331, 2023; Rossabi, *Khubilai Khan*, 54, 1988; Favereau, *The Horde*, 160-161, 2021.

**88** Atwood, *Encyclopedia of Mongolia and the Mongol Empire*, 202, 2004; Rossabi, *The Mongols*, 79, 2012.

**89** Saunders, *The History of the Mongol Conquests*, 117, 2001.

**90** Rossabi, *The Mongols*, 79, 2012. See also May, *The Mongol Empire*, 2018; Morgan, *The Mongols*, 2007.

**91** Rossabi, *The Mongols*, 78-87, 2012; Philipp and Haarmann, eds., *The Mamluks in Egyptian Politics and Society*, 2007.

**92** Dupuy & Dupuy, *The Harper Encyclopedia of Military History*, 422-424, 1993.

**93** See, for instance, Dupuy & Dupuy, *The Harper Encyclopedia of Military History*, 1993.

**94** Favereau, *The Horde*, 19, 2021.

**95** Favereau-Doumenjou, "New Collective Monograph," 921, 2016. See also Konukçu, "Berke Han" in İslâm Ansiklopedisi, 507.

**96**      Favereau, *The Horde*, 140, 2021. See also DeWeese, *Islamization and Native Religion in the Golden Horde*, 2010.

**97**      Year 1267 has also been cited for this event. See Harl, *Empires of the Steppes*, 347-348, 2023; DeWeese, *Islamization and Native Religion in the Golden Horde*, 2010; Benjamin, *The Mongol Empire*, 2021.

**98**      Favereau, *The Horde*, 113, 2021.

**99**      Morgan, *The Mongols*, 224, 2007.

**100**     See Konukçu, "Berke Han" in İslâm Ansiklopedisi, 507; Favereau, *The Horde*, 19, 2021.

**101**     Halperin, *Russia and the Golden Horde*, 29, 1987.

**102**     Vásáry, "'History and Legend' in Berke Khan's Conversion to Islam," 232, 1990; Konukçu, "Berke Han" in İslâm Ansiklopedisi, 506-507; Vásáry, "Orthodox Christian Qumans and Tatars of the Crimea in the 13th - 14th centuries," 271, 1988; Halperin, *Russian and Mongols*, 279, 2007.

**103**     For more on the peoples of the Steppes, see Taşağıl, *Bozkırın Kağanlıkları*, 2018.

**104**     See Favereau, *The Horde*, 163, 2021.

105      Ishayahu Landa in May and Hope, eds., *The Mongol World*, 653, 2022. See also Morgan, *The Mongols*, 2007.

**106**     See Galimov, "иСтория зоЛотой орДы И Церковно-орДынСких Отношений В СоветСкой иСториоГрАФии," 2016. See also Prawdin, *The Mongol Empire*, 2005.

**107**     DeWeese, *Islamization and Native Religion in the Golden Horde*, 93, 2010. See also Halperin, *Russia and the Golden Horde*, 1987.

**108**     Favereau, *The Horde*, 221-222, 2021.

**109**     See Vásáry, "Orthodox Christian Qumans and Tatars of the Crimea in the 13th - 14th centuries," 1988; Halperin, *Russian and Mongols*, 2007; Bawden, *The Modern History of Mongolia*, 1968.

**110**     DeWeese, *Islamization and Native Religion in the Golden Horde*, 90-135, 2010. See also Vásáry, "Orthodox Christian Qumans and Tatars of the Crimea in the 13th - 14th centuries," 271, 1988; Halperin, *Russian and Mongols*, 279, 2007.

**111**     See Favereau-Doumenjou, "New Collective Monograph," 921, 2016. See also Halperin, *Russia and the Golden Horde*, 1987; Bawden, *The Modern History of Mongolia*, 1968.

**112**     For details, see Kołodziejczyk, *The Crimean Khanate and Poland-Lithuania*, 2011; Benjamin, *The Mongol Empire*, 2021.

**113**     Hundley, *The Mongol Empire in World History*, 56-62, 2017. See also Halperin, *Russia and the Golden Horde*, 1987; Galimov, "иСтория зоЛотой орДы И Церковно-орДынСких Отношений В СоветСкой иСториоГрАФии," 2016.

**114**     Favereau, *The Horde*, 309, 2021. See also Galstyan, *Ermeni Kaynaklarına Göre Moğollar*, 2018.

**115**     See Favereau, *The Horde*, 161, 2021; Konukçu, "Berke Han" in İslâm Ansiklopedisi, 506-507.

**116**     Konukçu, "Berke Han" in İslâm Ansiklopedisi, 506-507. See also Juzjani, *Tabakât-i-Nasirî*, 1970.

**117**     See also Vásáry, "'History and Legend' in Berke Khan's Conversion to Islam," 230-252, 1990.

**118**     Konukçu, "Berke Han" in İslâm Ansiklopedisi, 506-507.

**119**     Vásáry, "'History and Legend' in Berke Khan's Conversion to Islam," 232, 1990. See also Hundley, *The Mongol Empire in World History*, 44, 2017; Favereau, *The Horde*, 162, 2021.

**120**     Vásáry, "Orthodox Christian Qumans and Tatars of the Crimea in the 13th - 14th centuries," 271, 1988; Halperin, *Russian and Mongols*, 279, 2007.

**121**     Following the assassination of Nawroz Khan, competing dynasties took control of the Golden Horde.

# Bibliography and Suggested Readings

*This is a very limited bibliography. Many more books and articles have been written on the Golden Horde and the Mongol Empire in general, but the ones listed here have either been consulted while preparing this biography, or would make for a useful reading on the topic. With a few Arabic, Turkish, and Russian exceptions, these sources are all either written in or translated into English.*

## Books

Aigle, Denise. *The Mongol Empire Between Myth and Reality: Studies in Anthropological History*, BRILL, 2014.

Al-Salaabi, Ali Muhammad. *Sultan Muhammad Al-Fatih* London, Al-Firdous, 2008.

Amitai-Preiss, Reuven. *Mongols and Mamluks: The Mamluk Ilkhanid War, 1260–1281.* Cambridge University Press, 2005.

Arnold, Thomas W. *The Preaching of Islam: A History of the Propagation of the Muslim Faith.* Forgotten Books, 2018.

Atwood, Christopher P. *Encyclopedia of Mongolia and the Mongol Empire.* Facts on File, 2004.

___. *The Secret History of the Mongols*. Penguin Classics, 2023.

Bawden, Charles R. *The Modern History of Mongolia*. Praeger, 1968.

Blair, Sheila. *A Compendium of Chronicles : Rashid Al-Din's Illustrated History of the World*. The Nour Foundation, 1995.

Broadbridge, Anne F. *Women and the Making of the Mongol Empire*. Cambridge University Press, 2018.

De Hartog, Leo. *Genghis Khan: Conqueror of the World* Tauris Parke, 2004.

DeWeese, Devin. *Islamization and Native Religion in the Golden Horde: Baba Tükles and Conversion to Islam in Historical and Epic Tradition*. Penn State Press, 2010.

Dupuy, R. R. Ernest, and Trevor N. Dupuy. *The Harper Encyclopedia of Military History*. HarperCollins; 4th edition, 1993.

Favereau, Marie. *The Horde: How the Mongols Changed the World*. Belknap Press, 2021.

Frashëri, Şemseddin Sami. *Himmat al-himam fiy nashr al Islam*. Mihran Matbaası, 1885.

Halperin, Charles J. *Russia and the Golden Horde: The Mongol Impact on Medieval Russian History*. Indiana University Press, 1987.

___. *Russian and Mongols. Slavs and the Steppe in Medieval and Early Modern Russia*. Editura Academiei Române, 2007.

Harl, Kenneth. *Empires of the Steppes: A History of the Nomadic Tribes Who Shaped Civilization*. Hanover Square Press, 2023.

Howorth, Henry H. *History of the Mongols (II)*. Longmans, Green, and Co., 1880.

Hundley, Helen. *The Mongol Empire in World History* Association for Asian Studies, 2017.

Jackson, Peter. *The Mongols and the Islamic World: From Conquest to Conversion*. Yale University Press, 2017.

___. *The Mongols and the West*. Routledge, 2018.

Jackson, Peter, translator. *The Mission of Friar William of Rubruck: His Journey to the Court of the Great Khan Möngke, 1253–1255*. Hackett Publishing Company, 2009.

Juvaini, Ata Malik. *Genghis Khan: The History of the World Conqueror*. Translated by J. A. Boyle, University of Washington Press, 1997.

Juzjani, Minhaj Siraj. *Tabakât-i-Nasirî*. Translated by Major H. G. Raverty, vol. 2, Oriental Books Reprint Corp., 1970.

Kaya, Mehmet, translator. *Moğolların Gizli Tarihçesi*. Kronik Kitab, 2018.

Khattab, Mustafa, translator. *The Clear Quran*. Book Of Signs Foundation, 2015.

Kołodziejczyk, Dariusz. *The Crimean Khanate and Poland Lithuania: International Diplomacy on the European Periphery (15th-18th Century)*. Brill, 2011.

Lyons, Jonathan. *The House of Wisdom: How the Arabs Transformed Western Civilization*. Bloomsbury Press, 2008.

May, Timothy. *The Mongol Empire*. Edinburgh University Press, 2018.

May, Timothy, and Michael Hope, editors. *The Mongol World*. Routledge, 2022.

Martin, Richard C., editor. *Encyclopedia of Islam and the Muslim World*: 2 Volume Set. 2nd ed., Macmillan, 2016.

Morgan, David. *The Mongols*. Wiley-Blackwell, 2007.

Morton, Nicholas. *The Mongol Storm: Making and Breaking Empires in the Medieval Near East*. Basic Books, 2022.

Philipp, Thomas, and Ulrich Haarmann, editors. *The Mamluks in Egyptian Politics and Society*. Cambridge University Press, 2007.

Polo, Marco. *The Travels of Marco Polo*. Translated by Henry Yule, Dover Publications, 1993.

Prawdin, Michael. *The Mongol Empire: Its Rise and Legacy*. Routledge, 2005.

Nicolle, David. *The Mongol Warlords*. Brockhampton Press, 1998.

Rashiduddin Fazlullah. *Jami uʾt-tawarikh: Compendium of Chronicles: A History of the Mongols Part One*. Translated and annotated by W. M. Thackston, Harvard University, 1998. Sources of Oriental Languages and Literatures 45; Central Asian Sources, 4.

Raven, James, editor. *The Oxford History of the Book*. First edition., Oxford University Press, 2023.

Rossabi, Morris. *Khubilai Khan: His Life and Times*. University of California Press, 1988.

___. *The Mongols: A Very Short Introduction*. Oxford University Press, 2012.

Saunders, J. J. *The History of the Mongol Conquests.*
University of Pennsylvania Press, 2001.

Taşağıl, Ahmet. *Bozkırın Kağanlıkları.* Kronik Kitab, 2018.

Weatherford, Jack. *Genghis Khan and the Making of the Modern World.* Broadway Books, 2004.

Wolfe, Diane. *Batu, Khan of the Golden Horde: The Mongol Khans Conquer Russia.* Genghis Productions, 2020.

**Articles and Online Resources**

Aasi, Joni, et al. "La Horde d'Or et l'islamisation Des Steppes Eurasiatiques." *Revue Des Mondes Musulmans et de La Méditerranée*, 2018, https://doi.org/10.4000 remmm.10234.

Aigle, Denise. "10 Legitimizing a Low-Born, Regicide Monarch. Baybars and the Ilkhans." *The Mongol Empire between Myth and Reality*, vol. Iran Studies, BRILL, 2014, pp.219–43, https://doi. org/10.1163/9789004280649_012.

Benjamin, Craig G. *The Mongol Empire.* Grand Valley State University, 2021. *The Great Courses.* Accessed 2024.

De Nicola, Bruno. "The Queen of the Chaghatayids: Orghīna Khātūn and the Rule of Central Asia." *Journal of the Royal Asiatic Society*, vol. 26, no. 1/2, 2016, pp. 107–20, https://doi.org/10.1017/ S1356186315000553.

D.R. Zaynuddinov. "Information on Genghis Khan, Berke, and Khan Uzbek in Bibliographic Collection of al-Safadi, Salah al-Din Khalil (d. 764 AH). Al-Wafi Bi al-Vafiyat (Complete Collection of Biographies of Deceased Persons or the History of al-Safadi)."

*Zolotoordynskoe Obozrenie = Golden Horde Review*, no. 4, 2015, 71–91.

Frazier, Ian. "Invaders: Destroying Baghdad." The New Yorker, 17 Apr. 2005, www.newyorker.com/ magazine/2005/04/25/invaders-3. Accessed 30 Oct. 2020.

Galimov, Teymur. *иСтория зоЛотой орДы И Церковно орДынСких Отношений В СоветСкой иСториоГрАФии.* Христианское Чтение, 2016, 329–43.

Il'nur Mirgaleev. "The Islamization of the Golden Horde: New Data." *Zolotoordynskoe Obozrenie = Golden Horde Review*, vol. 4, no. 1, 2016, pp. 89–101.

Konukçu, Enver. "Berke Han," *İslâm Ansiklopedisi*, Türkiye Diyanet Vakfı, https://islamansiklopedisi.org.tr/berke-han. Accessed in 2024.

Uludağ, Süleyman. "Seyfeddin Bâharzî," *İslâm Ansiklopedisi*, Türkiye Diyanet Vakfı, https://islamansiklopedisi.org.tr baharzi-seyfeddin. Accessed in 2024.

Favereau-Doumenjou, Marie. "New Collective Monograph: The Golden Horde in World History (Kazan: Sh.Marjani Institute of History of AS RT, 2016. 968 p. + 28 p. of Col. Ins.)." *Zolotoordynskoe Obozrenie = Golden Horde Review*, vol. 4, no. 4, 2016, pp. 918–23, https://doi org/10.22378/2313-6197.2016-4-4.918-923.

May, Timothy. "Ten Essential Women For A World History Class." *World History Connected*, 5.2 (2008): 39 pars. 25 Apr. 2024 https://worldhistoryconnected.press.uillinois.edu/5.2/may.html.

Mirgaleev, Il Nur. "The Golden Horde policies toward the Ilkhanate." *Zolotoordynskoe obozrenie = Golden Horde review*, no. 2, 2013, pp. 217–27.

"Ms Fr 2810 The Mongol Leader, Hulagu, Khan of the Ilkhanate Chases His Cousin, Berke, Khan of the Kipchak or Golden Horde in 1262, Forcing Him into a River, from Livre Des Merveilles Du Monde, c.1410-12 (Vellum) (b/w Photo)." *Bridgeman Images: The Bridgeman Art Library*, 2014.

Omar of the Orient. "How the sons of Genghis Khan converted the Mongols to Islam." *YouTube*, uploaded by 27 November 2023, https://www.youtube.com/watch?v=VkP3LUJE3pI.

Ölmez, Mehmet. "On Mongolian asara- 'to nourish' and Turkish aşa- 'to eat' from Middle Mongolian to Modern Turkic Languages." Festschrift in Honor of Andras J. E. Bodrogligeti, edited by Kurtuluş Öztopçu, vol. 7, Türk Dilleri Araştırmaları, 2007, p. 242.

Sayfetdinova, Elmira G. "The Personality of Sultan Baybars and His Role in Developing Relations of the Mamluk Egypt with the Golden Horde According to Arab Sources." *Zolotoordynskoe Obozrenie = Golden Horde Review*, vol. 5, no. 4, 2017, pp. 726–35, https://doi.org/10.22378/2313-6197.2017-5-4.726-735.

Sheremetyev, A. G. "Religious Aspects in Foreign Policy of the Golden Horde During Berke's Khan Reign." *Известия Саратовского Университета. Новая Серия. Серия: История. Международные*

*Отношения*, vol. 13, no. 3, 2013, pp. 3–8, https://doi.org/10.18500/1819-4907-2013-13-3-3-8

Vásáry, István. "'History and Legend' in Berke Khan's Conversion to Islam." *Aspects of Altaic Civilization III*, edited by Denis Sinor, vol. III, Bloomington, IN, 230-252, 1990.

___. "Orthodox Christian Qumans and Tatars of the Crimea in the 13th-14th Centuries." *Central Asiatic Journal*, vol. 32, no. 3/4, 1988, pp. 260–71. *JSTOR*, http://www.jstor.org/stable/41927889. Accessed 15 May 2024.

Yigit, Fatma Akkus. "Iktidar Ve Izdivaç: Memlûk-Altın Orda-Ilhanlı Üçgeninde Siyasi Evlilikler." *Karadeniz araştırmaları*, no. 49, 2016, pp. 103-.

# Acknowledgments

All praise and gratitude are due to the Creator who enabled me to bring together this oft-forgotten yet powerful story. I want to express my heartfelt appreciation to the many individuals who have offered their substantial support for this endeavor, including my family, friends, and mentors. First of all, many thanks to Stella Williams and Caitlin Dwyer for copy editing this brief work. Countless thanks to the following friends and mentors for their help and support in many of my endeavors: Burhan Fili, Didmar Faja, Brandon Mayfield, Abdullah Alkadi, Joel Hayward, David Jalajel, Amber Haque, Marwa Assar, Stef Keris, and Harry Anastasiou. My deepest gratitude also goes to Masud and Salma Ahmad, Mohammad Saeed Rahman, Mike and Linda Tresemer, Maqsood and Eloisa Chaudhary, Azim Haque, Kaan Katircioglu, Rania Ayoub, Imran Maqbool, Dana Lundell, Erzen Pashaj, Arbnor Rashiti, and the following families: Gashi, Bresa, Govori, Yavuz, Obaidi, Mirza, Jaffar, Shaheed, Mourad, Carter, Peyralans, Lipovica, Abazi, Qerimi, Ahmeti, Musliu, and many more.

I am also thankful to two great historians of our time, Jon Mandaville and Robert Harrison, two professors and mentors of mine who are no longer with us. They were the ones who inspired in me my love and deep appreciation for history.

## About the Author

Flamur Vehapi is a researcher, chronologist, poet, literary translator, academic, and success coach. He received his B.S. in Counseling Psychology with a minor in History from Southern Oregon University, and his M.A. in Conflict Resolution from Portland State University. Currently, he is an Education and Leadership Ph.D. candidate at Pacific University. In 2009, Flamur received the Imagine Award for Community Peacemaking. He taught social sciences at Rogue Community College and Southern Oregon University, after which he taught at various institutions in the Middle East. He has authored several books and translated two of Sami Frashëri's works. He has also worked as a contributing writer for the PSU Chronicles. Flamur and his family currently live in Oregon.

## About the Series

The *Impactful Lives* series delves into the biographies of essential and intriguing individuals, providing a critical examination of their accomplishments and contributions that set them apart as unique, influential, and enduring figures. This series explores the events that molded their lives and how they subsequently influenced our world, both historically and in the present times.

## About Crescent Books

Crescent Books is committed to publishing works that challenge the conventional and celebrate the diverse voices that enrich our understanding of faith, culture, and history. As a small, passionate team of book lovers, we guide authors through the publishing process with editorial freedom and genuine partnership. We serve our communities by producing books that inspire, provoke thought, and entertain, creating transformative reading experiences that connect with a broad audience and open doors to new perspectives on our ever-evolving world.

## Other Titles by Crescent Books

*The Book of Great Quotes* by Flamur Vehapi, 2025 (2nd. ed)

*A Breeze from the East* by Wael Almahdi, 2025

*When My Absence Becomes a Moon* by Laureta Rexha, 2024

*Grains of Destiny* by Brandon Mayfield, 2024

*The World According to Sami Frashëri* by Flamur Vehapi, 2024

*The Spectacular Escape* by Burhan Al-Din Fili, 2023

*Atheism Versus Belief* by Brandon Mayfield, 2023

*Kosovo: A Brief Chronology* by Flamur Vehapi, 2023

*Verses of the Heart: Poems* by Flamur Vehapi, 2021

*Ertugrul Ghazi: A Very Short Biography* by Flamur Vehapi, 2021

For our titles in other languages,
check out thecrescentbooks.com

Made in the USA
Columbia, SC
27 May 2025

58518761R00052